When Dragons Get Mad

By Pamela Little-Hayes, OTR/L

Illustrated by Katherine Mahon

To Debbie,
All my love!
Pamela Ng

This book is dedicated to Christopher, my very own Dragon and creative consultant, and to ALL my family for the love and joy that they bring to me.

Special thanks to Amy and Terry for their hours of work helping with editing and design.

Thanks to my co-workers and all the children at Cincinatti Children's Medical Center who inspire me every day.

Last but not least, thanks to Starbucks for almost always fueling my creative adventures, and in this case also helping me find my wonderful and talented illustrator!

What do Dragons do
when they are mad?

Do they break others' things, and throw their own toys?

Do they stomp and cry, and make lots of noise?

Should they pull people's hair?

Scratch, yell, or bite?

Should they unleash their anger and put up a fight?

Should these dragons go crazy and make a big stink?

Really, please tell me, what do you think?

They take a deep breath.
They take a time out.

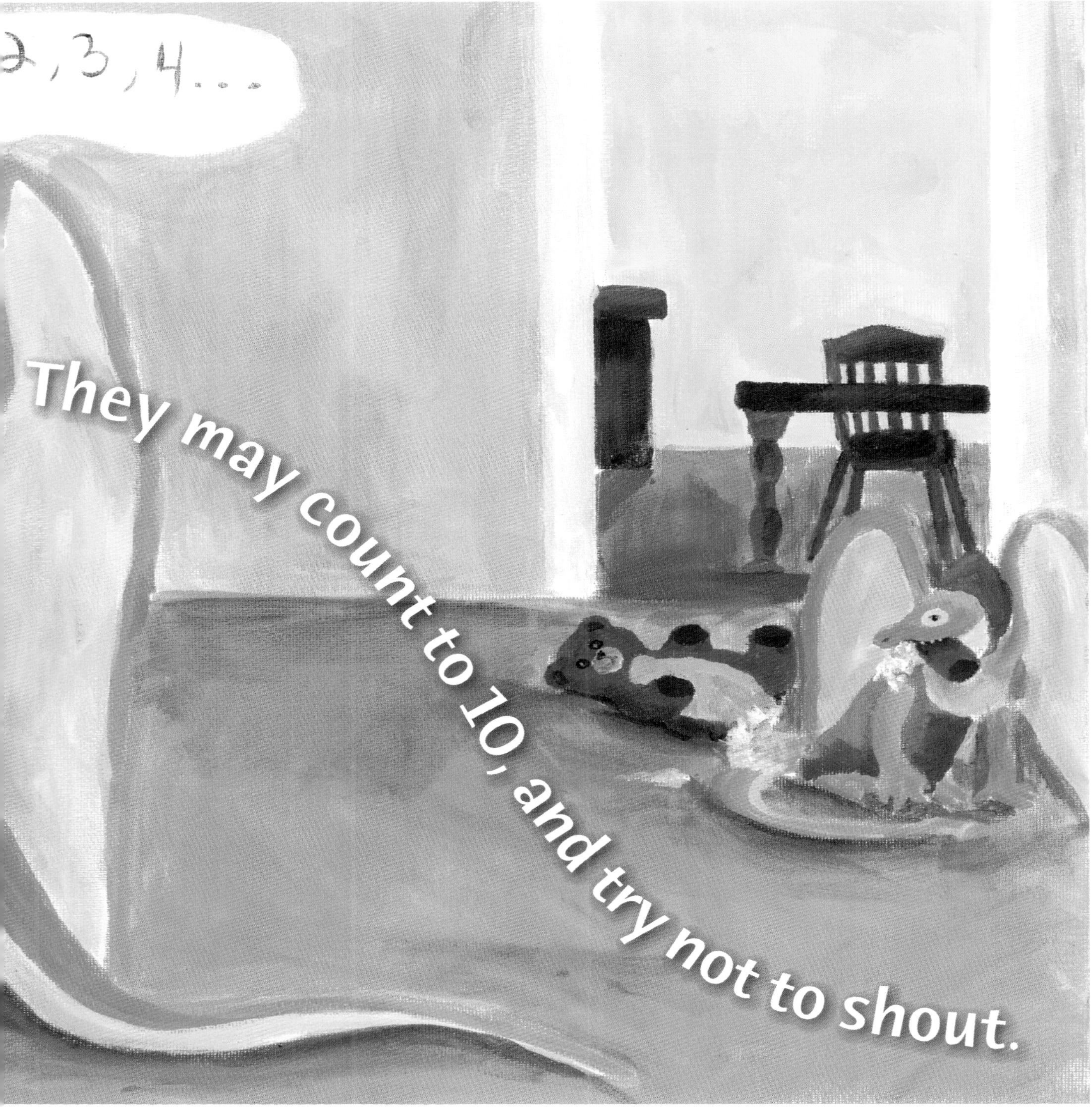

They may count to 10, and try not to shout.

They may ask for a hug, say "I need a break..."

… and then find a toy they can

squeeze, pull, or shake.

They may hide in some pillows

and dim all the light.

They are looking for ways

to make everything right.

Some like to swing, some like to sing...

They have to find out what's their special thing.

And soon they'll discover what works,

what's just right for them.

It's about finding ways to help stop the mayhem.

Then their anger calms down and
they can go on their way.

They begin to feel better
and have a good day.

What works for you?

This section of the book is designed for you and your child to explore and find calming strategies that work for you.

Once you find strategies that are helpful, cut out the pictures and place them on a key chain. You can bring them with you or place them on your child's book bag as a reminder of what you can do when your dragon gets mad.

Good luck, and have fun!

Take a Deep Breath

Ask For a Hug

Squeeze a Ball

Count to 10

Curl Up In a Blanket

Hide In Some Pillows

Swing In a Hammock

Yell Into a Pillow

Dim the Lights

Squeeze a Ball

Having a ball or squeeze toy available provides easy access to a calming tool. They can be placed on a backpack with a key chain or kept in a child's desk.

Ask For a Hug

Firm deep pressure can be very calming. A three second squeeze can help before escalation. Once a tantrum begins, longer hugs may be needed to help with calming.

Take a Deep Breath

Deep breathing is a great calming technique. It can be taught to very young children with the directions "smell a flower then blow out the candle."

Hide In Some Pillows

Having a designated soft enclosed space for calming can be great. It allows time to regroup, calm, and provides deep pressure and neutral warmth.

Curl Up In a Blanket

Blanket wraps are a great way to provide deep pressure and neutral warmth. For deeper pressure, roll your child tight like a burrito or baby swaddle.

Count to 10

Counting redirects attention and gives a break from the thing that has triggered the anger response.

Dim the Lights

Dimming the lights helps to decrease visual sensitivities and is relaxing.

Yell Into a Pillow

Yelling can be a great way to vent when you are angry, and it requires deep breaths. The pillow will not only muffle some sound, but also provide deep pressure to face and hands.

Swing In a Hammock

Slow swinging can be calming. Hammock swings also provide nice whole-body deep pressure.

Rock In a Chair

Swing

Do Pushups

Jump In the Air

Chew Some Gum

Listen to Music

Go For a Run

Pull On a Band

Go Wheelbarrow Walking

Do Pushups

Chair pushups—sitting in a chair and using your arms to push up—can be done easily in the classroom.

Wall pushups are done against the wall, becoming more difficult as you move your feet farther away from the wall.

Swing

Swings combine vestibular with deep pressure—especially when your child pumps the swing themselves. Swinging can be slowed as your child calms.

Rock In a Chair

Rocking chairs and gliders are great year round. They lend themselves to slower, more rhythmic rocking than swings.

Listen to Music

Music preference will play a large roll calming, but in general music that is softer and slow-paced tends to be calming.

Chew Some Gum

Resistive chewing—things like gum and gummies—provides resistive/heavy work to the mouth and can help calm and organize the body. Warm drinks and foods, resistive sucking with a crazy straw, or sucking a thicker liquid may also be helpful and calming.

Jumping

Jumping using a soft or rebounding surface like a trampoline can give added input.

Go Wheelbarrow Walking

Wheelbarrow walking, or walking on all fours like a bear, also provide great deep pressure and heavy work.

Pull On a Band

Stretchy bands provide resistance for pulling.

An old bicycle inner tube or bungee cord works, too.

Go For a Run

Going for a run gets you fresh air, exercise, and can be calming.

Taking a walk or bike ride—or just getting outside and moving—can provide some of the same positive calming rewards.

Community-based recreational activities to help keep your dragon calm.

Yoga
Yoga combines deep breathing, calming, relaxation, and exercise. There are many programs designed for children in the community and on DVD. Yoga can even be found in some video games.

Martial Arts
The Martial Arts combine movement, concentration, discipline, and exercise. Some programs, like T'ai Chi, are non-combative.

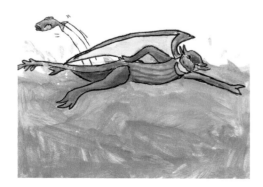

Swimming
Swimming provides deep pressure (like a hug) to the whole body. This activity can be enjoyed by everyone— even very young children.